SRA
OPEN COURT
READING

The Squirrel Plan

A Division of The McGraw-Hill Companies

Columbus, Ohio

www.sra4kids.com

SRA/McGraw-Hill

*A Division of The **McGraw·Hill** Companies*

Send all inquiries to:
SRA/McGraw-Hill
8787 Orion Place
Columbus, OH 43240-4027

ISBN 0-07-569493-X
    3 4 5 6 7 8 9 DBH 05 04 03 02

Quentin and Jen squint at the
squirrels in the park.
The squirrels are quick.

The squirrels squirm and squiggle far from
Quentin and Jen.
Jen has a plan.
She will make a banquet for the squirrels.

Jen puts corn, apples, and nuts on a bag.
She sets the bag on the aqua bench.

Quentin wants to help.
He will help quench the squirrels' thirst.
Quentin puts liquid in a pan.
He sets the pan on the aqua bench.

6

The squirrels quit squirming.
The smart squirrels gobble up the banquet.

Jen's plan was good.

TUDOR HALL:
THE BOISSEAU FAMILY FARM

Arthur W. Bergeron, Jr.